Today there are
sages to read. S
book?' This is not just another book but a journey of life experiences that we will all encounter in different ways and at different times. Will Kissinger has told us his experiences and the lessons we may all learn while on this journey called life. He has taken the complex encounters and made the learning simple.

As we travel these paths, it is always helpful to receive the wisdom of others' experiences as we ourselves meditate, listen to God's Word, and encounter the presence of our God. Knowing this author causes me to willingly recommend the pages of each chapter and challenge you to slow down, be aware of where you are, and welcome each of your own travels as a tool to enjoy this journey called life. May this book and the author's words light up the path for you, making your travels a bit more rewarding.

Enjoy the book and, most of all, enjoy life. After all, it is your journey!

—FRANKIE POWELL
Senior Pastor, World Outreach Center
Founder of Global Church Network

---

It is extremely trendy today to have a life coach guide you to a more successful, fulfilled 'you.' As a Christian, I have found the greatest life coach to be my heavenly Father, who leads me by his Spirit, through his Word.

Life is a process from beginning to end. Your walk with God is a process that is worth examining, enjoying, and celebrating. In *Journeys of Life*, through the partnership of contemplative journaling and studying God's Word, you can relish the special moments of your own life and learn to enjoy the presence of God in this rich process we call LIFE.

It's time to begin the journey.

—**DON CAYWOOD**
Pastor of Odessa Christian Faith Center

---

Will Kissinger does every follower of Jesus a huge favor by writing openly and honestly about what it means to walk out a life with Jesus. In order to understand this book better you need to know that the author is committed to live out what he says. Will has taken steps of faith and has sold out to Jesus, in more than just appearance but with his heart and life. His writings come from time with the Lord and fellowship with him. The reflections that are offered in these pages are an overflow of Will's relationship with an awe-inspiring God. You will be challenged and encouraged to see with fresh eyes that path that God has laid out for us, and the intimate relationship that he offers. Don't miss this opportunity to blaze a new trail in your walk with Jesus. I encourage you to take this journey towards a life with God that is available and waiting for us all.

—**MARK LEHMANN**
Senior Pastor, Cornerstone Church

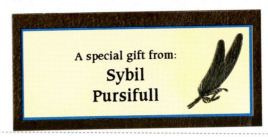

**A special gift from:
Sybil Pursifull**

# JOURNEYS OF LIFE

6/25/13

to Stephany

Hope this little book will be a help to you in life, and someday we can go back to Ireland again. Was a good time with you and Meghan.

# WILL KISSINGER

# JOURNEYS OF LIFE

### A THIRTY-DAY JOURNEY ON THE ROADS WE TRAVEL

**TATE PUBLISHING**
AND ENTERPRISES, LLC

*Journeys of Life*
Copyright © 2012 by Will Kissinger. All rights reserved.

---

No part of this publication may be reproduced, stored in a retrieval system or transmitted in any way by any means, electronic, mechanical, photocopy, recording or otherwise without the prior permission of the author except as provided by USA copyright law.

Scripture quotations marked (AMP) are taken from the *Amplified Bible*, Copyright © 1954, 1958, 1962, 1964, 1965, 1987 by The Lockman Foundation. Used by permission.

Scripture quotations marked (ESV) are from *The Holy Bible, English Standard Version®*, copyright © 2001 by Crossway Bibles, a publishing ministry of Good News Publishers. Used by permission. All rights reserved.

Scripture quotations marked (KJV) are taken from the *Holy Bible, King James Version*, Cambridge, 1769. Used by permission. All rights reserved.

Scripture quotations marked (MSG) are taken from *The Message*. Copyright © 1993, 1994, 1995, 1996, 2000, 2001, 2002. Used by permission of NavPress Publishing Group.

Scripture quotations marked (NCV) are taken from the *New Century Version®*. Copyright © 2005 by Thomas Nelson, Inc. Used by permission. All rights reserved.

Scripture quotations marked (NIV) are taken from the *Holy Bible, New International Version®*, NIV®. Copyright © 1973, 1978, 1984 by Biblica, Inc.™ Used by permission of Zondervan. All rights reserved worldwide. www.zondervan.com

Scripture quotations marked (NLT) are taken from the *Holy Bible, New Living Translation*, copyright © 1996. Used by permission of Tyndale House Publishers, Inc., Wheaton, Illinois 60189. All rights reserved.

The opinions expressed by the author are not necessarily those of Tate Publishing, LLC.

This book is designed to provide accurate and authoritative information with regard to the subject matter covered. This information is given with the understanding that neither the author nor Tate Publishing, LLC is engaged in rendering legal, professional advice. Since the details of your situation are fact dependent, you should additionally seek the services of a competent professional.

---

Published by Tate Publishing & Enterprises, LLC
127 E. Trade Center Terrace | Mustang, Oklahoma 73064 USA
1.888.361.9473 | www.tatepublishing.com

Tate Publishing is committed to excellence in the publishing industry. The company reflects the philosophy established by the founders, based on Psalm 68:11,
*"The Lord gave the word and great was the company of those who published it."*

Book design copyright © 2012 by Tate Publishing, LLC. All rights reserved.
*Cover design by Kate Stearman*
*Interior design by April Marciszewski*

---

Published in the United States of America

ISBN: 978-1-61862-670-7
1. Religion / Christian Life / Devotional
2. Religion / Christian Life / General
12.04.02

# A PORTION FROM THE PROCEEDS

of this book will go to support missionaries Joil and Leah Marbut, who, with their four children, are changing the nation of Ecuador one day at a time.

Joil and Leah have been working together with the Shuar Indians in Ecuador for twelve years. In that short time, they have planted dozens of churches in villages and communities that have previously never heard the gospel of Jesus Christ. They have founded a Bible institute that ministers to native leaders and pastors. The Marbuts also started a program called "Fundación Vida Internacional," which helps meet the needs of the communities they serve in. Fundación Vida gives them the help they need to start and build schools, educate community health promoters, and continue to install water filtration systems while maintaining the existing ones that serve thousands. They have also started a scholarship program that is helping to break the cycle of the exploitation of young Shuar ladies.

> For this is what the Lord has commanded us: "I have made you a light for the Gentiles, that you may bring salvation to the ends of the earth."
>
> Acts 13:47 (NIV)

# TABLE OF CONTENTS

| DAY | | |
|---|---|---|
| | Introduction | 13 |
| 1 | Letting Go and Diving In | 15 |
| 2 | Giving and Receiving Forgiveness | 21 |
| 3 | Everything | 27 |
| 4 | Loving Hands | 31 |
| 5 | Prodigal Son | 35 |
| 6 | Unchanging God | 41 |
| 7 | Faithful | 47 |
| 8 | When I Think of You | 51 |
| 9 | His Love | 55 |
| 10 | Sin's Flag | 61 |
| 11 | Puppets Act | 67 |
| 12 | Living in Last Chances | 73 |
| 13 | A Broken Life | 79 |
| 14 | Two Masters | 85 |

| 15 | All-Sufficient Grace | 89 |
| --- | --- | --- |
| 16 | He Paved The Way | 93 |
| 17 | Unending Love | 99 |
| 18 | One More Round | 105 |
| 19 | Temporary Setbacks | 111 |
| 20 | Redemption | 117 |
| 21 | Mile after Mile | 123 |
| 22 | Undeserving | 129 |
| 23 | Inseparable | 133 |
| 24 | Don't Let Go | 137 |
| 25 | None Like Him | 141 |
| 26 | My Enemy | 147 |
| 27 | The Choice Is Yours | 151 |
| 28 | Confessions | 155 |
| 29 | Heaven's Sake | 161 |
| 30 | The Journey of Life | 167 |
|    | Conclusion | 173 |

# INTRODUCTION

We all have a journey; it's life. While each of us is different in where we came from and how we got to the place we are today, we have one thing in common: we are all involved in this thing called life. Our own personal journeys are different, but I believe the roads we travel in this journey are very much the same. We all have traveled the roads of success and failure, hurt and pain, rejection and acceptance, love, hate, loss, freedom, bondage, regret, disappointment, and encouragement. The rate at which we've traveled these roads varies in all of us. While some have experienced success more than failure and others failure more than success, we all have experienced both. It's only the degree of your experience that makes your journey different from mine.

This book is written for you, the reader. These are my journeys, the roads I've traveled. I pray this blesses you and, at the same time, challenges your life to be the best it can be now without waiting. I want you to read this book and realize who God created you to be. Realize what you have the right to as a son or daughter of the Creator of the universe. You are entitled to more than you know. Remember, you have all that God is within you, so be encouraged to live and never be afraid to journey.

> Herein is our love made perfect, that we may have boldness in the day of judgment: because as he is, so are we in this world.
>
> 1 John 4:17 (KJV)

**DAY 1**

# LETTING GO AND DIVING IN

Surrounded by my options
Which one will I take?
Do I want it all, do I want some
Or do I want just a taste?
In the past a taste seemed
　to satisfy my soul
But as I got to know you more
I wanted as much as I could hold
Now I look back I hold
　nothing at all
It's been dropped as I
　stumble and trip
As I fall and fall
What happened to the things
　you've given me?
Whatever happened to my
　heart of integrity?
Now all I live is a life of insanity
I'm the lowest of low in
　all of humanity
My heart's cry is deeper still

Even through all my mountains
    and all my hills
If climbing's what it takes to
    get me deeper with you
Then I'll give it my best and
    that's what I'll do
I'm wading in the water yet
    I fear its depths
Longing to dive in but only
    taking baby steps
The water's cold and I'm not
    sure what to expect
What's holding me back?
Cause everything I've ever had I've lost
What's keeping me from you?
Whatever it is I'll pay the highest cost
I'm taking this risk and letting go
God be my keeper
Anoint my life and fill my hands
As I go deeper

Sometimes we limit God—we limit what he wants to do for us, in us, and through us. I remember a sermon I heard while attending a discipleship program called "Master's Commission." In that sermon, those there were encouraged to not limit God but to dive into him.

I've realized through the years that I have limited what God can do in my life for many different reasons, whether it be not tithing, lack of prayer and reading his Word, or simple disobedience. It has caused me to miss out on what God had for me and delayed the fulfillment of his purpose and destiny for my life. I want all that he has for me, and I don't want to miss out on any of it. I don't want to just pray when I need something or tithe when I'm in financial trouble. I don't want God to just be my get-out-of-jail-free card. I want him to be my everything every day!

God wants us to let go—let go of our hurt, pain, insecurities, fear, pride, and lack of trust. He wants you and me to surrender it all, to not just wet our feet but dive into all that he is in us. It's only then that he can be all that he is through us.

> [For my determined purpose is] that I may know him [that I may progressively become more deeply and intimately acquainted with him, perceiving and recognizing and understanding the wonders of his person more strongly and more clearly], and that I may in that same way come to know the power out flowing from his resurrection [which it exerts over believers], and that I may so share his

sufferings as to be continually transformed [in spirit into his likeness even] to his death, [in the hope] That if possible I may attain to the [spiritual and moral] resurrection [that lifts me] out from among the dead [even while in the body]. Not that I have now attained [this ideal], or have already been made perfect, but I press on to lay hold of (grasp) and make my own, that for which Christ Jesus (the Messiah) has laid hold of me and made me his own. I do not consider, brethren, that I have captured and made it my own [yet]; but one thing I do [it is my one aspiration]: forgetting what lies behind and straining forward to what lies ahead.

Philippians 3:10-13 (AMP)

In what ways have you limited God in the past? What things in your life are you holding back?

_____

_____

_____

_____

What needs to take place in order for you to surrender these things and dive totally into him?

_____

_____

_____

_____

What are some ways you can remind yourself daily to stop for a moment and evaluate yourself and see if you are trusting in yourself or in the God who loves you?

_____

_____

_____

_____

## DAY 2

# GIVING AND RECEIVING FORGIVENESS

The mercy of God is so great
For who else would forgive
And forget all our mistakes?
I've been caught in sin
By men who've desired
    to kill me
But there's something about
    the ways of God
As he decides to heal me
My accusers argue as they
    throw me at his feet
But what better place
    could I be?
Though I'm shamed
    I find such peace
They're waiting for his answer
Rocks in their hands
Yet my deliverer pays
    them no mind
As he kneels to write in the sand

The mob grows impatient as
    they wait for a reply
And I begin to wonder is this the day
That I'm condemned to die?
But when he had finished
I knew I was going home
his gentle voice was so comforting
As he said, "Let him with no sin
Cast the first stone"
My heart almost burst from my chest
The tears streamed down my face
As one by one the rocks
    fell to the ground
I knew once again I'd been
    saved by grace
He lifts up my head with so
    much compassion
And looks me in the eyes
"Where are your accusers?" he asks
As he wipes the tears that I've cried
"Today is the day of salvation
I've given you a new start
Not only have I wiped the
    tears that you've cried
But I also wiped the sin from your heart
Now go on your way

And serve me your Lord
But as you go remember
To go and sin no more"

The greatest thing to me about this story is not that the woman was forgiven but that Jesus would have done nothing different if she was brought before him again and again for her sin (John 8:1-11). He would have again said, "Let him with no sin cast the first stone," and he would have bowed to that shameful woman and lifted her head with no less love and compassion as he did the day before, and again, he would have said, "Go and sin no more." In fact, if that woman had been brought back to Christ an innumerable amount of times, he would have still said the same words and would have still shown that woman the same love and compassion that he had shown her the first time he forgave her.

How do I know this? I know this because Christ has done it over and over again. He has repeated those same lines and actions to me and to you that he said and did to the "adulterous woman" some two thousand years ago. Think about it! How many times has he lifted your head from its shameful state and said, "Go and sin no more"? How many times has he turned away your accuser, just like he turned away the angry mob that day, leaving you alone so that he can minister to you? You know that God has forgiven you over and over again. Some of you are still trying to overcome things in your life, and every day you find yourself being thrown at his feet, but every day it's the same thing: "Let him with no sin cast the first the stone" and "Go and sin no more." Every day his love for you is the same, and his compassion to forgive your sins is never lessened over time. Because I can testify of Christ's unfailing mercy, despite the times I've asked again and again for mercy, I can say that he would have done the same thing for that woman over and over again until she got it right. You know that he has forgiven you countless times, and he will continue to do so until you or even I get it right.

To me, that is the greatest thing about this story. Knowing this woman would always find mercy at the feet of Jesus, even if the whole town refused to forgive her, Christ would have still wiped away her sins, her guilt, and her shame if she allowed him to.

> If we claim to be without sin, we deceive ourselves and the truth is not in us. If we confess our sins, he is faithful and just and will forgive us our sins and purify us from all unrighteousness.
>
> 1 John 1:8-9 (NIV)

In what ways have you experienced the forgiveness of Christ?

_____

_____

_____

_____

What does it mean to you knowing God's forgiveness and mercy will never change in your life?

_____

_____

_____

_____

Are there relationships you have where you need to exercise forgiveness? If so, with whom?

_____

_____

_____

How can you remind yourself to daily walk in God's forgiveness without taking it for granted?

# EVERYTHING

**DAY 3**

You are the holy King
   of all creation
You are the sovereign Lord
   of my salvation
You are every part of
   my very being
You are the comfort in
   my mourning
You are the wings that send
   this heart soaring
You are everything to me
You are the light when
   my world is dark
You ignite a flame in my soul
God, you are the very spark
I want you more than life itself
I cherish you, Lord
In my time of need you
   are my help
You are my best friend the
   lover of my soul
You are my mark yes
   my very goal
You are everything to me

My Father is the founder of this world, the one who established the universe. He put the sun, the moon, and the stars in the sky. He is the most powerful being on earth, richer than anyone who will ever live. I have free access to him any time of day or night. He looks out for my best interests and has destined me for greatness. He loves me unconditionally; he encourages me and cheers for me. He picks me up when I fall. He holds me when I'm sad and wipes every tear when I cry. He is never too busy to be involved in my life. He is my biggest fan. He's everything I've ever wanted in life. He's my source of life, the reason I live. I'm filled with excitement every morning when I wake up. I can't wait to experience the journey he has planned for me. I can't wait to experience the blessings, the joy, the peace, and the victory with each new day. I live for him; without him, I'm nothing. What a wonderful life I get to live; what a wonderful journey I get to travel. I hope you're experiencing all that he is. I hope today you're letting him be your everything.

> Take delight in the Lord, and he will give you your heart's desires. Commit everything you do to the Lord. Trust him, and he will help you. He will make your innocence radiate like the dawn,

and the justice of your cause will shine
like the noonday sun.

> Psalm 37:4-6 (NLT)

What does God mean to you?

_____

_____

_____

_____

How can you take delight in him and his ways on a daily basis?

_____

_____

_____

_____

We say all the time, "God is my everything," but how does your life's outlook change when you say, "I mean everything to God"?

_____

_____

_____

_____

If you're not experiencing the fullness of who God is in your life, why do you think that is, and what changes can you make to enjoy all that he is every day?

_____

_____

_____

_____

# LOVING HANDS

**DAY 4**

The gentle hands of my
    loving Father
They hold my hands in
    every step I take
They hold my hurts,
    failures, and desires
And throw away the
    wrongs that I make
Gentle enough to wipe
    every tear from my eye
Yet tough enough to fix me
When in him I don't abide
Never calloused only strong
From carrying my
    burdens for so long
The hurtful words, the
    horrendous deeds
Every thought that evil feeds
The very things that have
    scarred your hands
Broke your body and
    made you bleed
Yet all these things are
    hard to see

> They're covered by the blessings
>   you've given me
> My sins are forgotten and
>   I've been set free
> Now I live a life of hope I'm
>   not afraid to dream
> My heart is open and I'm
>   ready to receive
> Everything your hands long to do for me

It is such a blessing for me to get up and know that God has my whole day under control, that this day, the day he predestined me to live, is in his hands. It's not true that "He Holds the Whole World in His Hands." I wish it were, but it's just not. God can only hold what's been given to him. He can only control what we surrender to him. I remember when I tried to still hold on to things in my life, things I thought I could do on my own, things I wanted to control. What a mess those pieces of my life were. I juggled and struggled in those areas all the time. I'm not sure why we try to accomplish and overcome things on our own. I think we just don't trust God. I know that was my reason. It's that fear in us that if our hands are not in it then it won't work out the right way. I'm not sure why I thought my hands could do what his hands could. My hands will fail, but his will not. There's nothing my hands can do that can come close to what his hands can do. My hands are just human, but the hands of God are supernatural, unfailing, mighty hands that never lose control. There was a time where God had my heart but not my life. I tried to do things my way, but I've learned to take my hands off my own life and allow him to hold all of me every day.

> Indeed, he loves his people; all his holy ones are in his hands. They follow in his steps and accept his teaching.
>
> Deuteronomy 33:3 (NLT)

List some personal things you believe the hand of God has done in your life.

_____

_____

_____

_____

Knowing that God holds your life in his hands, how does that change your daily perspective of a new day when you get up each morning?

_____

_____

_____

_____

What things in your life are you still holding on to that you need to place in his hands?

_____

_____

_____

_____

# PRODIGAL SON

**DAY 5**

There was a man who
    had a friend
That would give him anything
    his heart desired
Yet this man only took
    advantage of him
And in the end
Burned him like a fire
This friend was so much
    closer than any other
For this man considered
    him his brother
But with the pass of time the
    man broke his heart
And slowly yet steadily
    they drifted apart
However, the friend never
    left the man's side
Yet followed him day and night
Hoping to restore what had died
His arms were always open
He was always beckoning
    and calling

The friend was there in the
    man's successes
And even caught him while
    he was falling
Despite the man's attempts
To ignore his friends good deeds
He finally came to the realization
That this friend was all he'd need
So he turned around to ask forgiveness
For all he had done
But before he had a chance
The friend embraced him with a hug
"Don't worry, my child,
    I've forgiven you,"
That's what my friend said to me
"I forgave you before you hurt me
And I'll forgive you for eternity"

This is the story of those in Christ who simply turn his or her back on him, doing his or her own thing. It's the story of the prodigal son, who took his inheritance and spent it all. Returning home, thinking he could possibly be a servant in his father's household, his father ran out to meet him, putting a ring on his finger, and then he held a feast to celebrate his son's return (Luke 15:11-32). This is exactly what Jesus does. You discover his love and you enter into a relationship with him, but you, somewhere along the line, decide to do your own thing. So you leave, not knowing, though, that he hasn't left you. He follows you, still loving you and still helping you when you give him the opportunity to. In the end, you realize that he was more of a friend and more fulfilling than anyone or anything you tried. Before you have the chance to ask forgiveness, he is already there to give you his free grace, much like that father who rushed out to the fields, calling for his son when he saw him in the distance. Before his son could say a word, his father was already there.

> Then Jesus told them this parable: "Suppose one of you has a hundred sheep and loses one of them. Does he not leave the ninety-nine in the open country and go after the lost sheep until he finds it? And when he finds it, he joyfully puts it on his shoulders and goes home. Then he calls his friends and neighbors together and says, 'Rejoice with me; I have found my lost sheep.' I tell you that in the same way there will be more rejoicing in heaven over one sinner who repents than over ninety-nine righteous persons who do not need to repent."
>
> Luke 15:3-7 (NIV)

Where were you in life when you decided to turn to your heavenly Father?

_____

_____

_____

_____

What thoughts cross your mind realizing that all of heaven celebrated your return?

_____

_____

_____

_____

"He will never leave you nor forsake you." What words could you express to God, knowing he's always been there for you, even when you tried to do life on your own?

_____

_____

_____

_____

# UNCHANGING GOD

**DAY 6**

I look at the cards that
    I've been dealt
I've been through thick and thin
With no one there to help
Most of the time I was down
Because no one seemed to care
Yet even when I felt alone
I know you were still there
You never left my side
Though I couldn't feel you
You are always my guide
Though I can't see you
You've caught every tear
That's rolled down my cheek
When no one else would
You tucked me in bed and
    sang me to sleep
When I was scared
You were my comfort
When I was angry
You were my peace
You provided when I
    was in need
You were my strength

When I was weak
God, I've been through a lot
But it's made me who I am today
My life story I've used
To break the devil's chains
The cards I hold are worth
    the saving of a soul
It's let me trust in you
And made my heart as pure as gold
So God, don't ever let me
Get discouraged at who I am in you
Though the devil attacks me
There's one thing I know is true
There are a lot of things
The storms of life can change
But there's one thing that stays the same
It's that you're still God

When I wrote this, I was thinking of a friend of mine whose life growing up was not as easy as others. My friend didn't have a good family life; he even lost his leg due to health problems at an early age. Despite what life handed him, my friend overcame his setbacks and became one of the most joyful, encouraging people in my life. I think he realized that God loved him and wanted the best for his life. God didn't give him those problems, and when he allowed him, God replaced his hurt and sense of failure with dreams, hope, and an excitement about living.

A lot of you are like my friend. Sure, you may have both your legs, but life has dealt you things that you have deemed unfair. You have said, "Why me?" as you fight the feelings of anger and bitterness and hurt. God is not the author of your pain, but he desires to be the end of it. If you, like my friend, will surrender those things of your past to him, he will give you the future you've always imagined. God is for you! He loves you! He didn't cause your problems; he came to fix them. Life will always happen, even after you surrender it to him, but I can assure you he wants the best for you. He will give you a better life than you could have imagined. Circumstances will come and go, life will change and change again, but the God who loves you and wants to help you will always be there. He never changes! You may get hurt again or face another setback, but the God who fixed it all will continue to heal and fix you as long as you continue to allow him. He will always be God!

> There should be a consistency that runs through us all. For Jesus doesn't change—yesterday, today, tomorrow, he's always totally himself.
>
> Hebrews 13:8 (MSG)

How has God fulfilled your life and been what you needed when family and friends failed?

_____

_____

_____

_____

What do you think about knowing that the loving, life-changing God you fell in love with will always be the same loving, life-changing God?

_____

_____

_____

_____

God wants to give you an excitement about living. What would a new excitement about life do for you?

_____

_____

_____

_____

# FAITHFUL

**DAY 7**

Lord, when I think about you
And what you've done for me
So much joy floods my heart
When I found you, Jesus,
 you set me free
You took away all my sins
And gave me a fresh start
Though it's been hard and I
 can't say I haven't fallen
Your arms were always open
Your voice was always calling
Beckoning me to come to you
To give my everything
Though sometimes I
 didn't hear it
And at times I chose not to
You never gave up on me
You never even thought to

Think about how faithful God is. We don't deserve anything he has given us, but he still gives it. For all the times in my life that I've messed up and done wrong, he still loves me. David said, "The Lord is good, and his love endures forever." He was so right. God is good, and his love will never fail. God should have walked away a long time ago, but he didn't because he's faithful. Even though I've cheated him so many times, he's still by my side.

We all have forgotten him so many times, yet just like he was to David, he is to us. He's good. To me, what's so great is not that he hasn't forgotten us, like at times we have him, but that he's never even wanted to. He's so in love with us! He's so for us! The thought of not pursuing us is not in him!

> Give thanks to the Lord, for he is good!
> His faithful love endures forever.
>
> Psalm 136:1 (NLT)

In what ways has God been good to you?

_____

_____

_____

_____

How do you feel knowing that he will always love you?

_____

_____

_____

_____

What are your thoughts knowing God has never even thought about giving up on you?

_____

_____

_____

_____

# WHEN I THINK OF YOU

**DAY 8**

In the quietness I think of you
So much joy floods my soul
For you've taken my life
    with its broken pieces
And refined them into pure gold
You lifted my head when it
    was bowed in shame
Forgave my sins and
    took my pain
You've given me a reason
    to be happy
I know I shouldn't cry
Yet in the quietness I
    think of you
So many tears flood these eyes
I don't deserve what
    you've given me
God, I don't deserve anything
I should be forgotten
    deserted and left to die
Yet you treat me like a king
Despite my wrong

> You continue to bless me
> Despite my rejection
> You continue to accept me
> I love you more than this life
> And I will serve you till the end
> That's the least I can do
> > for my best friend

I cannot explain how happy I am when I think about Jesus and what he has done for me. He took my life that was worthless and broken, and he perfected it. I was so shameful and full of sin, yet he knelt down and lifted my head high to a prideful position, forgiving and removing all the cracks, flaws, and fragments of my life. When I think of all he's done for me, I could cry uncontrollable tears of joy because I deserved absolutely none of it. When I should have been treated like a worthless dog, he chose to call me a friend and a son. No matter how many things I have done wrong in my life, his blessings outweigh them all. I can't begin to count how many times I turned my back on him, yet I know he has accepted me just as many times. I love him so much, and I know that there is no way I could not follow in his ways. I put him before anyone in my life because he means more to me than anyone ever could. He's my companion forever, my best friend, and I will remain in him for eternity.

> God is faithful (reliable, trustworthy, and therefore ever true to his promise, and he can be depended on); by him you were called into companionship and participation with his Son, Jesus Christ our Lord.
>
> 1 Corinthians 1:9 (AMP)

When you think about what he has done for you, what does it make you want to do?

_____

_____

_____

_____

Sometimes we forget that our relationship with him is eternal. How does it make you feel knowing you and God will be together forever?

_____

_____

_____

_____

Knowing God is faithful and can be depended on unlike any other causes you to do what?

_____

_____

_____

_____

# HIS LOVE

"Crucify him! Crucify him!"
    It echoes still today
Do you hear the rings
    that hatred brings
Of the day you felt such pain?
I envision the crowd
    I see the cross
As if I was there myself
I imagine the pain the
    heaviness of your heart
Yet still no cry for help
I begin to shiver as I see the
    blood trickle down your face
Across your body to the ground
    pooling at the cross's base
I hear the mockers and
    their remarks
Are you the Son of God?
The world anticipates
    the answer but you
    never even nod
The hammer's pounds
    are as clear
As the thumping of my heart

**DAY 9**

Ripping flesh, cracking bone
I can pinpoint every part
I can feel the wetness of every tear
Enough to flood an ocean
The wailing cries of your followers
Who've showed so much devotion
Darkness covers the face of the earth
Demons anticipate your death
They wait and watch and
    hold their breath
Only to lay your soul to rest
I see your body as it hangs between
    those wooden beams
Yet the image I perceive is transformed
And a new you is revealed to me
No longer a man beaten and bruised
    but a king in all his glory
Where the world thought
    that this was the end
It was really the beginning of the story
I see a robe and a sash
    revealing who you are
In place of thorns a golden crown
Shining like the brightest star
Now I know how much you love me
Now I truly understand why

How could anyone not serve you?
Only a fool would not try
As I see you gasp for one last breath
I myself uncontrollably cry
"Father, into your hands I
 commit my spirit,"
You say as you die

Christ really does love us. He died on the cross—a cruel and torturous death—so that we might have life and have it more abundantly than we ever imagined. I know that those who condemned him and thought he deserved to die were relieved when he breathed his last breath. Those who followed him to the end and mourned as he left this earth were heartbroken that their king was dead. But the crucifixion was definitely not the end; his robe of royalty and his crown of salvation had undoubtedly been there the whole time. The world thought they had this "Jesus character" out of their hair for good. Some thought the best thing to ever happen had just been removed from their lives, but if they had looked harder, they would have seen that Christ's death was just the beginning.

I'm firmly convinced that Christ thought of me and you as he hung there. I can't think of a single reason why anyone would not take the eternal life he has to offer. He died a horrible death so that you, me, and every other person to ever walk this earth, might accept eternal life and be redeemed from paying the price for their own sins. Don't think twice about serving him—there's nothing to think about. He hung on that cross that all your sins, burdens, struggles, sicknesses, and diseases may be lifted from your shoulders. Only a fool would not take the salvation and freedom from sin that Christ offers so freely for his or her own life. Don't hesitate and waste the blood that was shed for you. I pray that you accept him and all he wants to bless you with. Ask Jesus to forgive you of your sins and invite him to be the lord of your life because he laid down his life for you.

> For while we were still weak, at the right time Christ died for the ungodly. For one will scarcely die for a righteous person—though perhaps for a good person one would dare even to die—but God shows his love for us in that while we were still sinners, Christ died for us. Since, therefore, we have now been justified by his blood, much more shall we be saved by him from the wrath of God.
>
> Romans 5:6-9 (ESV)

What kind of commitment would you show to someone who willingly would lay his or her life down for yours?

_____

_____

_____

How would you respond to someone who knew you were condemned to die yet told you they wanted to die in your place so that you could live and experience life?

_____

_____

_____

What are you doing with your life to show Jesus that what he did was worth it?

_____

_____

_____

_____

# SIN'S FLAG

Why do I do what I don't
 want to? I'll never know
Why do I always follow
 the current and never
 fight the flow?
Why am I always pulled to the
 ground forgetting your face
Crawling toward sins banner
 and forgetting your grace?
Juggling temptations of
 quitting this race
I slow the run, I slow the
 walk, I slow the pace
Pulled against my will I
 can make out the flag
Do I reach out and touch the
 pole? Do I dare risk a grab?
Just as I try I run into a wall
It pauses these evil desires long
 enough to hear your call
I read the bricks each
 one has a name
Vision, prayer, my reputation
 to maintain

**DAY 10**

Accountability, scripture,
>   worship from my heart
The things built up in me to keep
>   us from drifting apart
The force to wake me from
>   the pied piper's tune
To turn me around and back toward you
I know I'll always be tempted to
>   turn away from you, Lord
But I have something to fight with
It's that my heart is spoken for

There is a sin nature that has pulled us all at one time or another in our lives; perhaps it's pulling you now. See, while the sin nature is gone, that hypnotizing call that sin has is still there, and if you listen to it, sin will pull you away from Christ and make you crawl toward its banner. The flag of sin is different in us all. We all struggle in different areas of life. The most important thing you can do is first identify that flag because, even if you don't want to sin, that piper's tune will cause you to forget everything but the seductive flap of sin in the wind. Once you've discovered the weaknesses in your life, you will know how to pray and better guard your heart and mind against that gravitational force called sin! I have found in my life that the more I pray and read my Bible, the farther away that flag becomes. My desire for a relationship with Christ drives the desire for sin farther away. It's the time we spend together in his Word and in prayer that builds this wall in me.

I'm not perfect and never will be, but I can learn to master my struggles and not let them master me. It's the excitement of walking in what he's given me, enjoying the benefits of knowing he has spoken for my heart and called me his own. It's the feeling of freedom that I'm reminded of every day as we journey together that keeps me from sin. If I decide not to pray and fill my life every day with his Word, that pied piper playing sin's anthem gets louder and louder. It's like Alex the lion in *Madagascar*. He's a friend of a zebra, and as long as he gets his daily dose of meat at the zoo, he doesn't know he's not supposed to have a zebra for a best friend. But when Alex and his friends end up on an island and he doesn't eat for several days, he begins to go crazy and doesn't know why. He tries to eat his friend on several occasions, and he can't control himself. He becomes hypnotized and is overtaken by the call to eat meat. He fights against himself to not eat his friend because his body is craving to be filled. As long as I feed on what I'm supposed to—God's Word—that call to fill my life with sin will not, unless I allow it to, overtake me. If you find yourself obeying the call to sin, perhaps you haven't eaten any spiritual meat and your body is hungry. Every day your spirit wants to be filled with something. Don't fill it with God and it will find something to fill it with. Establish a real relationship every day with prayer and God's Word because without it you will be just like Alex—lost, hypnotized, and hungry.

> The sinful nature wants to do evil, which is just the opposite of what the Spirit wants. And the Spirit gives us desires that are the opposite of what the sinful nature desires. These two forces are constantly fighting each other, so you are not free to carry out your good intentions.
>
> Galatians 5:17 (NLT)

What does the banner of sin look like in your life?

_____

_____

_____

_____

What steps are you taking to tune out the call of sin in your life?

_____

_____

_____

_____

What are some things in your life that will discourage you from sin?

_____

_____

_____

_____

# PUPPETS ACT

Play the song pull my strings
Watch me dance and
    hear me sing
Lower the curtain only
    to raise it again
Day in and day out
Does this ever end?
I'm an entertainer but
    only to death
I work at the hypnotizing
    theater
For the down and depressed
Where every guest must
    be with evil obsessed
I'm the puppet who
    steals the show
With each kick and
    every arm throw
I captivate my audience
They're on the edge
    of their seats
I'm as messed up as all my guests
But with every try at escape
I feel the power of defeat

**DAY 11**

> I'm tired of playing this game of charades
> When you think you're free
> Are you still just a slave?
> A slave to the master of
>     puppets of this world
> Or is your master Jesus
> The only one who cares?
> Mine is the master of this
>     world the one of death
> But Lord, untie these strings
> I lay this career to rest
> Set me free of this puppet's act
> Give to me everything that
>     this world has stolen
> God, I ask you
> Give it all back

I can't help but think of that part of the movie *Pinocchio* where he is on the stage and the crowd is cheering. He loves it, but after a while, he realizes it's not what he thought, and when he tries to escape, the man won't let him. Is it not the same way in life? We are living outside of Christ, and we are having so much fun. After a while, though, we realize that it is not what we expected and in the end is not what we wanted to do. We try and get away, but our master won't let us. He tries to hold us prisoner and use us as a puppet to entertain this world. How many of you can relate your own life to that of Pinocchio's? You were once having so much fun doing your own thing, yet it wasn't as fulfilling as you thought it would be. You realized you wanted to do something else, but when you went to quit, you found out that you really weren't in control of your life at all—the devil was. You see, Pinocchio had no strings. Well, in the end, he found out there were some strings attached after all. The devil is a liar who will never tell you the truth; sometimes we don't even realize it, but we are a slave to him and his theater, this world. The only way you can escape the charades that you play in life is to ask Jesus to set you free. Allow him to be the lord of your life and he will untie those strings, restore what the devil took from you, and give you the life you have been looking for.

> So, since we're out from under the old tyranny, does that mean we can live any old way we want? Since we're free in the freedom of God, can we do anything that comes to mind? Hardly. You know well enough from your own experience that there are some acts of so-called freedom that destroy freedom. Offer yourselves to sin, for instance, and it's your last free act. But offer yourselves to the ways of God

> and the freedom never quits. All your lives you've let sin tell you what to do. But thank God you've started listening to a new master, one whose commands set you free to live openly in his freedom!
>
> Romans 6:15 (MSG)

How did you wake up and see that what this world offered you was just a lie?

_____

_____

_____

_____

How were you shown the way of escape from the god of this world?

_____

_____

_____

_____

What can you do to wake up those around you who are hypnotized by this world?

_____

_____

_____

_____

# LIVING IN LAST CHANCES

**DAY 12**

I hung on that cross
Sentenced to die for
   my sinful life
My death would be no loss
But this man who
   hangs beside me
What wrong has he done?
Show me the sin in his heart
So great that God would
   black out the sun
This man is no sinner but
   the Son of God
The teacher, preacher,
   and healer
Greater than any priest in
   all the synagogues
I can feel it in my spirit
The peace he brings to
   this wretched place
I can hear freedom
   ringing in my ears
I can see it written on his face

> Thank You, God, for one
>     last chance for grace
> I've done a lot of things to
>     hang my head in shame
> Yet in this final moment I'm
>     going to gain a new name
> I believe you're the Lord, Jesus Christ
> You said, "Believe in me and
>     you shall be saved"
> So rebuild this broken life
> And remember me beyond the grave

The man hanging on the cross beside Jesus wasn't asking him to make a mental note of who he was. He was really saying, "Put me back together. Take the broken pieces of my shattered life and make me whole." "Remember me, Jesus," was a cry from this man's spirit because something told him that Jesus was different. He said, "Remember me," because he knew that the power of life and death, the power of mercy, grace, and forgiveness, was in this man. I don't know if the man knew who Jesus was, if he was there when Jesus fed the five thousand. I don't know if the man heard Jesus sit in the square and tell a parable or if he saw the crippled man by the pool of Bethesda get up and walk away from his mat. I can't tell you the personal history of the thief on the cross, but I do know that in all the pain God gave him control of his senses long enough to hear his spirit speak. The man didn't have anything to lose—no friends to mock him and turn their back on him, no spouse to leave him for his newfound faith. This man wasn't even concerned with peer pressure. He was on the verge of death, and whether that was the Son of God or not who hung beside him, he said, "I have nothing to lose. I'm going to die, and if there truly is life after death, then I want to be in the right place. So whether you're the Son of God or not, I've got to say, 'Jesus, remember me,' in the few minutes I have on this earth. 'Restore me.'" The man saw a chance, and he wasn't going to pass it up.

How many times have we seen the chance yet passed it up? If we could just live our lives like the man beside Jesus and say, "I have nothing to lose"; if we could say, "God, I'm going to ask you to put me back together. Please remember me"; if we lived every moment of our lives like it was our last chance for grace, like that man so desperately did in his death, then we would never pass up Christ. We would be about our "Father's business" at all times, never to wander to the right or the left, never to miss the call of God on our lives.

Live every moment like it's your last, live for Christ like you have nothing to lose. Ask him to remember you, to put you back together. Then take the wholeness that he so graciously bestows on your life and walk in it for as long as you live.

> So be very careful how you live. Do not live like those who are not wise, but live wisely. Use every chance you have for doing good, because these are evil times. So do not be foolish but learn what the Lord wants you to do.
>
> Ephesians 5:15-17 (NCV)

In what ways did he put you back together?

_____

_____

_____

_____

If you lived every day of your life like it was your last day to live, what would you do tomorrow?

_____

_____

_____

_____

If you found out you only had thirty days to live, what things would you change in your life?

_____

_____

_____

_____

# A BROKEN LIFE

**DAY 13**

How wonderful your arms as
 they hold me through my life
How good it was to be
 in your ways
And to have your presence
 all day and every night
There was so much joy that
 I had when I was in you
At times I long for that
 peace that I once knew
How I struggle inside
 fighting against myself
 to gain it all back
While I immerge deeper in sin
Trying to numb the conviction
 of the godly life I lack
But I can't ignore what's been
 branded on the inside
I try so hard to bury the mark
 of God but it won't die
Every night I dream I'm
 the prodigal son
Leaving this life I've chosen and
 back to your arms I run

> Yet when I awaken I'm still
>     my same old, dirty self
> To ashamed, stubborn, prideful,
>     and scared to cry out for help
> I say I'm finally happy, I can be
>     myself, and I'm doing fine
> Yet I can't describe how horrible,
>     disgusting, and worthless
> I really feel on the inside
> I want so badly to return to you
> But I don't know how to start
> I've taken what you've given me
>     and I've torn it apart
> And as much as I don't deserve you I
>     can't get the thought out of my mind
> So perhaps I will return to you
> But we will only know with time

I cannot understand how you can have a relationship with God, live as one with his son, and one day just walk away from it all. I know there are many of you who are reading this who can relate. You walked with God, talked with God, and knew and had a personal relationship with his son, Jesus, but you decided to do your own thing. I know that every night when you lay your head down on your pillow, you try to fight the truth that is on the inside of you. I know you know you are in sin, and I know you know that God is real. Why don't you do what you know in your heart of hearts is right and repent of your sins, turn, and follow Christ? I know you realize that what you found in Christ is what you so desperately need in your life, so place him back in your life; be that prodigal son or daughter you dream of being. Let him wash away your guilt, your hurt, and the pain that you placed in your life as you veered off course. He still loves you, and he's still for you. He is calling for you today to let him back into your life. Don't wait, don't hesitate, and don't feel ashamed, embarrassed, or afraid. Do it now! Do it while you have the chance. Allow him to free you from the prison you've placed yourself in. God's love is unending, and it doesn't matter how far you've fallen, how many times you've fallen, or even how hard you've fallen. He still has a plan for your life, and it's a plan to prosper you and not to harm you; it's a plan to give you a hope and a future. He formed you in your mother's womb with a specific plan. It's not too late to fulfill what he has called you to do. Please, if you're reading this and it fits your life, then return to the Lord. Don't wait another day because tomorrow may just very well be too late.

> So repent (change your mind and purpose); turn around and return [to God],

that your sins may be erased (blotted out, wiped clean), that times of refreshing (of recovering from the effects of heat, of reviving with fresh air) may come from the presence of the Lord.

Acts 3:18-20 (AMP)

What things in your life do you need to repent of?

_____

_____

_____

_____

Do you know someone who has stepped out of the arms of God? What are you doing to help them return?

_____

_____

_____

_____

What worldly things were you involved in that you thought you couldn't live without if you surrendered to Christ?

_____

_____

_____

_____

# TWO MASTERS

I feel your love it's so warm
I'm aware of your shelter
  from these storms
Your arms are my strength
Your voice is my guide
Your grace my redemption
  for the evil I've tried
What will it take for you to
  have my entire heart?
How many times do you have
  to give me another start?
You are what I need
  most in this life
Yet I still forget you
You have been more to me than
  any other could ever be
Yet I still forsake you
You can't serve two masters
Yet we try every day
Living for God one minute
Then the next minute living
  the worldly way
God, help me to both love
  you and hate evil

**DAY 14**

> For with that comes faithfulness
> With that comes a pure heart
> With that comes success
> I never need another start

The Bible says that no one can serve two masters; he will both hate the one and love the other or he will stand by and be devoted to the one and despise and be against the other (Matthew 6:24). So many people are looking for help from the storms of this life. They're in desperate need of escape from this world and all that it is. Yet when the only one who can really give them satisfaction that will last forever and not just for a season tries to help, they reject it. The only one who is going to give you joy and fulfillment you want and need is Christ. *Love* the Lord and *hate* evil. God watches over you, and he will preserve your life and deliver you (Psalm 97:10). Ask him to give you clean hands and a pure heart, and when you put all these things into play in your life, you will truly have fulfillment and everlasting joy and peace. When you fully give all that you are to him, you will find yourself wanting for nothing because everything you have ever sought after will be found in him who gave his all for you.

> O you who love the Lord, hate evil;
> he preserves the lives of his saints (the

children of God), he delivers them out of the hand of the wicked.

Psalm 97:10 (AMP)

In what ways have you tried to serve God and something else in your life?

_____

_____

_____

_____

How complicated was it to serve two masters, and what problems arose from living that life?

_____

_____

_____

_____

How did you come to finally surrender to one master?

_____

_____

_____

_____

# ALL-SUFFICIENT GRACE

Everything's going right but how long will it last
Because I know every time I'm doing good
I fall right back into my past
My life is a ship in a constant raging storm
Crashing up and down on the waves I've created through my scorn
My anger a fierce wind that seems to buffet my sail
The rain every tear that falls for every time I've failed
But you've built me to last for I've never been shattered
Somehow I make it through with a lost crew and a sail that's tattered
O' what a morning
When your glory like the sun shines across my sea

DAY 15

> What joy floods my soul
> When you calm the storm
> > and you forgive me
> And I know through all I've done
> Your grace is sufficient
> No matter what I do your
> > mercy is endless
> So hold me in yours arms till I
> > breathe my last breath
> Nothing can separate us not even death
> For I'm committed to you and
> > you're committed to me
> And this commitment will last
> > from now even into eternity

"He has removed our sins as far from us as the east is from the west" (Psalm 103:12, NLT). All that you and I have regretted doing in our lives—our mistakes, our failures, sin—God has erased it! We are the reason we have trouble doing right. It's not our past; we don't have a past. We are a new creation. It's simply us. We will always have temptations, but we will also always have the choice to give in or not. Most of the storms of life can be avoided if we follow his commands. Yes, life will still happen, there will be some things we can't control, but God gave us the recipe for life. If you bake a cake and don't follow the recipe exactly, that cake will not be as good. It will still be edible but not as easy to swallow. It's the same in life. We have a God-given recipe for a great life, but if we leave an ingredient out—say prayer or the Bible—we will still get life; it just may not be as pleasant to chew. The good news is you get to bake 365 days a year. Today's recipe wasn't great, and I forgot a few of the ingredients, but there's always going to be an opportunity to include all the ingredients for a better life tomorrow.

> Oh, the joys of those who do not follow the advice of the wicked, or stand around with sinners, or join in with mockers. But they delight in the law of the Lord, meditating on it day and night. They are like trees planted along the riverbank, bearing fruit each season. Their leaves never wither, and they prosper in all they do.
>
> Psalm 1:1-3 (NLT)

How do you feel knowing God doesn't remember your sins?

_____

_____

_____

What ingredients do you need to add or take away from your life recipe in order to have the life he came to give you?

If you were feeding yourself the wrong kind of spiritual food, what could you do to make sure you get the proper serving of God every day?

# HE PAVED THE WAY

3 P.M.
6/22/13
Ireland

Yea though I walk
   through the valley
Of the shadow of death
I will fear no evil
For I know that you
   walked it first
And at the end of that
   path was the key
The key to set us free
   from sin's curse
Though it's hard and I'm
   beaten and bruised
My source of strength
   is remembering
Everything you went through
So I press on knowing I
   have nothing to lose
What can I lose that you
   haven't lost already?
My friends, my family,
   pride, my life

**DAY 16**

> You gave everything on that
>     cross as a sacrifice
> How comforting to know we've
>     walked the same road
> You with your cross me with this load
> Tracing your footsteps down
>     the same trail
> Following the drops of blood
>     and fallen nails
> That lay beside the path
>     created by your cross
> I finally realize the price you paid
> How much it cost
> To lay down your life on
>     the hill of Calvary
> To hang before the world
>     and claim victory
> And to think you did it just for me

I've realized that I'm not going to walk through anything in life that he hasn't walked through already—not persecution, rejection, betrayal, pain, hurt, or even temptation. Jesus faced every struggle and problem that you or I will ever deal with in our lifetime. The only difference is he took captive every thought and he used the Word of God to overcome every situation. He didn't dwell on the problems or the struggles he faced.

He didn't get scared at his circumstances or feel sorry for himself. He stood on the Word of God in all situations. Why did he do that? He did it for you and me, to show us that we can, in him, be more than a conqueror. Christ is with you and wants to help you with your life journey. If you would just listen to him and allow him to work through your life, you would see that he's paid the price and life doesn't have to be hard. He wants you to walk down that path and lay your cares at the cross because it was there that he journeyed some two thousand years ago and he took care of this thing we call life.

> Could it be any clearer? Our old way of life was nailed to the cross with Christ, a decisive end to that sin-miserable life—no longer at sin's every beck and call! What we believe is this: If we get included in Christ's sin-conquering death, we also get included in his life-saving resurrection. We know that when Jesus was raised from the dead it was a signal of the end of death-as-the-end. Never again will death have the last word. When Jesus died, he took sin down with him, but alive he brings God down to us. From now on, think of it this way: Sin speaks a dead

language that means nothing to you; God speaks your mother tongue, and you hang on every word. You are dead to sin and alive to God. That's what Jesus did.

Romans 6:6-11 (MSG)

Christ has experienced everything you will walk through today. How will this fact change the way you look at today's events?

_____

_____

_____

_____

Having a relationship with Christ brings God down to your level. How can you face life situations differently now?

_____

_____

_____

_____

What words could you express to a Savior who laid his life down for you and me so we could live eternally?

_____

_____

_____

_____

# UNENDING LOVE

Corrupted, deceived,
    and led astray
The story of my life
Raised in church know God
Yet still can't do what's right
Am I a lost cause?
'Cause every day I fall
Sometimes I'd give anything
    just to end it all
If there's more then show
    me, I know there is
I'll do anything to be rid
Of my past, present, and
    things of tomorrow
Going down fast, no
    time for sorrow
I cry and cry, but to no avail
And I wonder if you
    still feel the nails
Every time I fail
It gets harder to climb
    back on my feet
Instead of pushing forward,
    I want to retreat

**DAY 17**

> But I move on
> Even when it seems everything
> > is going the opposite way
> My mark is you the price is paid
> It's not easy being a Christian
> Whoever said it was is a liar
> Take from me, God, my sins
> And cast them in the fire
> Now I thank you for a life
> > that resembles you
> And a pure heart that will remain true

I've been in church all my life, yet sometimes I struggle doing the things that in my heart I know are right. I truly understand Paul when he said, "What I want to do, I don't do, but what I hate to do, this I keep on doing." Paul was no different from any other man or woman, boy or girl that ever walked this earth. Why is it that I do the wrong things sometimes instead of doing what in my heart I know I should do? Why do we as humans compromise our faith to dabble in the pleasures of sin, knowing the consequences? Why do we constantly ruin our lives with a temporary pleasure that is only fun for a season? We will never find anything more satisfying and pleasing than what we've found in Christ, so why de we turn to other sources to find our satisfaction and pleasures?

There have been times when I've wanted to give up this journey that Christ and I started, but where could I go to find what I found in Christ? I know there are many of you who can relate to what you're reading now. Take it from someone who's been in your shoes: Don't quit. Don't throw in the towel because the storms of life that you yourself created are crashing on your shores. The Bible says in Psalm 30:5 that those storms will not last always, but joy will come in the morning, so press on to know him, follow hard after him. Christ loves all of us despite our sin. It's not an easy road to walk—the road of Christianity—but it's so worth it. No matter how deep into sin you've fallen, Christ is always there with his arms open wide, longing for you to return to him. Don't think he's forgotten you because you have sinned. I've been there. I have made tremendous mistakes that have hurt me and people I love deeply, but in the end, God was still there telling me he loved me and he was proud of me. I can't take those days, events, and mistakes back, and you can't either. That doesn't mean we stop or give up on our journey. It simply means we make things right with God, those we've hurt, and ourselves. Learn from mistakes, no matter how big or small, and implement your newfound knowledge to tomorrow's journey. Christ's love is an indescribable, endless love with no boundaries to sin. He will always love you and will always be proud of you, so if you need to make things right, do so today, right now, while you have the chance.

> Because one person disobeyed God, many became sinners. But because one other person obeyed God, many will be made righteous. God's law was given so that all people could see how sinful they were. But as people sinned more and more, God's wonderful grace became more abundant. So just as sin ruled over all people and brought them to death, now God's wonderful grace rules instead, giving us right standing with God and resulting in eternal life through Jesus Christ our Lord.
>
> Romans 5:19-21 (NLT)

What have you learned from the mistakes you have made?

_____

_____

_____

_____

Are you making the same mistakes over and over again? What do you need to do to rid yourself of those mistakes?

_____

_____

_____

_____

How do you feel knowing that God will never leave you and will always love you?

_____

_____

_____

_____

# ONE MORE ROUND

How many times have I given in
When I've heard the devil's lies?
How many times have
   I disbelieved
Not even caring to try?
I can't begin to count
The times I've almost died
The times I've listened
   to Goliath
And left God's side
I search for my fight but I
   can't find it anywhere
My giants have stolen it and
   replaced it with fear
There go my dreams,
   visions, and desires
There goes everything to
   me that I hold dear
I want to be what you've
   called me to be
But here I am still bound
If I'm going to be the
   best of the best

**DAY 18**

> Then I know I've got to
>     go another round
> I've got to stand to my feet
> And knock the devil down
> Proclaim your Word and speak to the sea
> Move my mountains and claim victory
> Let me be a David
> And believe in whom you've
>     called me to be
> For who am I?
> I'm a child of God
> And who are you?
> You're my phenomenon

How many times have we as believers given in to the lies of the devil? How many times has the devil said you were no good and you couldn't accomplish anything in your life? When he's told you that no one loves you and you're worthless, did you believe him and give up on your dreams? When he whispered in your ear that you were a failure, did you try to successfully do anything with your life anymore? The devil is a liar! Everything he says to you goes directly against what God has promised to you. The devil says you're sick, but God says by his stripes you have already been healed. The devil whispers that you are all alone and no one cares about you, but God says he will stick closer than any brother.

The devil says you're broke and you can't pay your rent and you can't feed your kids, but God says, in 2 Corinthians 8:9, "Christ became poor, that through his poverty you could become rich." Just like he paid the price for our sins and our sickness and diseases at the cross, he paid for our financial freedom as well. Maybe you've had a hard time letting go of the mistakes you've made and you can't shake the feeling that God hasn't forgiven you of the things you have done, but he's told you in his Word, "There is no condemnation in him that is in Christ Jesus." Or perhaps you feel like you are not loved, but that also is a lie because his love endures forever. He is your healer, your provider, the supplier of *all* your needs. He's your lifelong companion who will never abandon you, not even for a second, in your life. He's the forgiver of *all* your sins. He's your strength, source of life, encourager, savior, and everything you will ever need. So why is it that we listen to the devil? Why is it that we take his negative word over the promised Word of God? Why do we believe what the devil tells us? Why do we back down in the corner, too afraid to fight for what we know is true?

I think somewhere along our journey we all have lost the spirit of fight at one time or another. We just get tired of the devil; we get tired of standing in faith. I heard a story where someone once asked the heavyweight boxing champion of the world how he became a champion. He said late in the match when he was just too tired to fight, too tired to swing his arms, too tired to throw another punch and his eyes were swollen and his head was pounding, he would encourage himself and cause the spirit of fight to stay with him by saying four little words: just one more round. God wants you to stand up and encourage yourself. Tell yourself, "Just one more round." Let that spirit of fight come alive in you again. Find that promise God gave you, that weapon against what the enemy is telling you, and say it over and over again. Encourage yourself with God's Word, his weapon for you against the enemy.

> And that about wraps it up. God is strong, and he wants you strong. So take everything the Master has set out for you, well-made weapons of the best materials. And put them to use so you will be able to stand up to everything the devil throws your way. This is no afternoon athletic contest that we'll walk away from and forget about in a couple of hours. This is for keeps, a life-or-death fight to the finish against the devil and all his angels.
>
> Ephesians 6:10 (MSG)

List how the enemy has tried to defeat your faith in life.

_____

_____

_____

_____

List how you were determined to fight and you saw the hand of God strengthen you and bring you to victory:

_____

_____

_____

_____

If you were someone who had lost their spirit to fight, what could you do to cause that spirit to rise back up in you?

_____

_____

_____

_____

# TEMPORARY SETBACKS

I'm trying to press in
But no one will let me
What do I have to do
To be set free?
God I've battled these
    things all my life
And I'm not leaving here
    without a fight
No matter how dumb I look
Or what they say about me
Today is the day of victory
They're anxious to see
    what you'll do
But, God, if they would
    just let me pass
I could grab my breakthrough
They surround you so tightly
    that I can't even see
But my spirit tells me
    you're there
I've lost all sense of dignity

---- DAY 19

> Just to be close to you is my only care
> With my last ounce of strength
> I throw myself at the crowd
> I hear them murmur in disgust
> To each other aloud
> Who is this person, what are they doing
> God, if they only knew the
>     touch of your robe
> Was all I was pursuing
> I reach out in despair and grab my goal
> Knowing my faith in the Master
> Has made me whole

What an amazing story this is, how this woman battling an "issue of blood" for twelve years was convinced, despite the efforts of her past, that if she only touched the clothes that he had on, she would be healed. She could have so easily looked at her results of all prior efforts at finding a cure and simply said, "No, this won't work either." She didn't, though; she'd had so many failed attempts in her life at finding healing, but she wouldn't give up. No doctor could give her what she looked for. No one had an answer to her problem, even after she sold all she had to find a cure. She didn't dwell in her setback but instead trusted in God. Because she set her faith and hope in the Lord, she found the answer she so desperately sought out and

God gave her a comeback in her life that outweighed any setback she had or would ever know.

Setbacks in life will come, but if we will not look at our situation but look instead to our answer for the situation, God will meet our need. He's moved by our faith in him, not by our troubles and problems. God will always take care of your situations when you trust in him and believe he is working it out. This is exactly what this woman did in Matthew 9:20, Mark 5:25, and Luke 8:43. She could have said, "Nothing's worked before, so why should it work this time?" but she didn't. She could have blamed God for her problem, but she didn't. She could have thought, and might have, of a million reasons to not follow that crowd and risk another chance at failure that day, but she chose not to listen. You know what I love so much about this story? Mark 5:25 says that she kept telling herself over and over again, *If I could only touch his garment, I will be healed.* She convinced herself of it and said it so much it was in her heart, her mind, and her spirit. She wasn't running up, screaming, "Master, come quickly!" or "Have mercy on me." She didn't need to cause a big scene; her plan was to simply touch that coat he wore and walk away, but she didn't make it unnoticed. Jesus, realizing power had come out of him, asked, "Who touched me?" The disciples replied, "What do you mean? The whole crowd is pressing against you on every side!"

Everyone was touching him, and it wasn't easy to get to him because of the multitude following him. This woman believed that if she touched his coat, she would be healed; she was convinced of it, but she had to fight for it. I'm sure that crowd didn't just part and say, "Oh, here comes Jane. Let's let her touch his garment." She had to push and shove and probably got knocked down by the crowd that was pushing and shoving to get closer too. I'm sure people gave her a look of disgust, as if she was butting in on their opportunity to touch him. But her desperation and determination outweighed her pride. With all her strength and in her pain and misery, she went ahead and fought for it and pushed through that mob to get close to Jesus to touch his garment. When she did, because she believed it, power left him and entered her, making her whole.

It doesn't matter your situation, how bad it is, or how long you've struggled with it. God doesn't want you to be so full of stress and worry and pain. He has freed you from those things. He wants so badly to let you enjoy that freedom, but he won't just take your problems. He wants you to give them to him. He wants you to believe he can and will take care of you. He wants you to stop feeling sorry for yourself and stop wallowing in all that's wrong in your life. He wants you to reach out and touch him like that woman did. Put your faith in him and see if he doesn't make you whole.

> Jesus replied, "Truly I tell you, if you have faith and do not doubt, not only can you do what was done to the fig tree, but also you can say to this mountain, 'Go, throw yourself into the sea,' and it will be done. If you believe, you will receive whatever you ask for in prayer."
>
> Matthew 21:21-22 (NIV)

What setbacks has the enemy given you in your life?

_____

_____

_____

_____

List the comebacks that God gave you because you didn't give up:

_____

_____

How can you overcome any disbelief in your life about God setting you free from the setbacks you are experiencing?

# REDEMPTION

Your hand reaches to the
   darkest depths
As your blood washes my body
You pull my being from
   the clutches of death
I dance before you now
As joy floods my once
   lifeless soul
I was a wretched, blind,
   dirty beggar
Yet you looked deep within
And somehow saw a
   glimpse of gold
I never thought someone
   would pick me up
And wipe the dirt from my face
Yet here I am
Proudly I stand
And free to walk in grace
Death, where is your sting?
Grave, where is your victory?
The power of sin has no
   hold over my life

**DAY 20**

> For the death of my King
>> has delivered me
> Rising from the dead
> He rebirthed my condemned life
> Healed my broken wings
> Now I soar to the highest heights
> I have a freedom that I've
>> never known before
> A joy and a peace that was only found
> When I found Jesus my Lord
> After everything you did for me
> You finally got my attention
> I thank you every day
> That my life is a testimony
> To the power of redemption

Where would we be right now if it wasn't for the cross? If it weren't for the power of redemption, that life-changing infilling of the Holy Spirit, where would we be? Dead? Alone? Lost? Hurting? Sick? Broken? Dying? We no doubt would be in different places, but one thing is for sure: we would all be in need! We would be in need of healing, restoration, guidance, love, freedom, grace, forgiveness, hope, life, joy, peace, and all the benefits that come with the acceptance of Christ as our Savior. Without him, we have none of those things, yet with his redeeming blood, we are in need of nothing! With his obedience to the cross, you and I have total fulfillment through grace. A pastor friend of mine defines grace as this: "God having already done everything for us that we would ever need." See, in him, we need nothing. At times we feel we have nothing, yet through his spirit that abides in us, we have everything we will ever need already! What a revelation! I am in need of nothing that through Christ's obedience hasn't already been met. Through redemption, I have all I need to live this life for Christ the way God intended me to live.

> Praise be to the God and Father of our Lord Jesus Christ, who has blessed us in the heavenly realms with every spiritual blessing in Christ. For he chose us in him before the creation of the world to be holy and blameless in his sight. In love he predestined us to be adopted as his sons through Jesus Christ, in accordance with his pleasure and will— to the praise of his glorious grace, which he has freely given us in the One he loves. In him we have redemption through his blood, the forgiveness of sins, in accordance with the riches of God's grace that he lavished on us with all wisdom and understanding.

> And he made known to us the mystery of his will according to his good pleasure, which he purposed in Christ, to be put into effect when the times will have reached their fulfillment—to bring all things in heaven and on earth together under one head, even Christ.
>
> Ephesians 1:3-10 (NIV)

What does the word *redemption* mean to you?

___

___

___

___

Describe the power of redemption that took place in your life.

___

___

___

___

What can you do to share the power of redemption every day with those you know who need to experience redemption for themselves?

_____

_____

_____

_____

# MILE AFTER MILE

This is an endless road that
    I've walked upon
I can't take another step
The scorching heat has
    burnt my brow
It's left me exhausted to
    the point of death
Yet it quickly fades as fast
    as the sun can set
And my eyes adjust to the
    darkness of night
The blackness surrounds
    me with its thick mass
I could cut it with a knife
The clouds have formed a
    pod directly overhead
I brace myself for the
    stinging rain
It drenches my body it
    burns my skin
Leaving my joints with pain
These winter winds go
    right through me
To the very depths of my soul

**DAY 21**

> Yet I forget all about it as
>     numbness takes control
> I've trudged through mud
> Waded the floods
> And endured the snow
> I ignored the bumps the bruises
>     the stiffness and the pain
> Pushed on through the heat
>     the winter and the rains
> I've simply had enough
> Enough of every horizon
>     looking the same
> I'm on my knees crying out
>     from this dreadful place
> Have you seen my Lord?
> Have you seen my embrace?

I know many of you feel like this is an endless road and no matter how long you've been walking it, you feel like you're seeing the same horizons day after day, month after month, and maybe even year after year. In my life, there were three things that made me feel this way. One, I had sin in my life, simple as that. I was doing things I knew were wrong. Two, I did not have a relationship with Christ; he was my Savior, but not my Lord. How do you expect to live in Christ if you never talk to God? What if I told you I had a best friend and we spent every waking moment of every day together but we never said one word to each other? How strong do you think our relationship would be? I'd never know who my friend was! When we pray, it deepens and strengthens our relationship with him. It's so important that you have a prayer life. A friend of mine once sent me a birthday card that said, "A man is only as big as his prayer life." Though I didn't immediately "up" my prayer time, I never forgot what he wrote. And last but not least, number three: reading God's Word. Everything you will need for life is on the pages of that book. If you want to actually get somewhere on this road and see a different horizon, then you have got to study the map.

I cannot describe how important these things are for your life. If you will start to pray and read God's Word, obeying what he reveals to you, every day you will see the horizons of your life begin to change. If you pray and read God's Word every day, you will begin to recognize the sin in your life and your friend, God, will help you overcome your temptations. Life is easier when you put God in it. Make him number one in your life, do what he says, and see how quickly it makes a difference in your everyday living. Jesus came that we might have life, not just be able to breathe or to merely survive, but a life that is overflowing, a life that is abundant. The only way to tap into that abundance in your spirit is to begin living in your spiritual life every day.

> Now, if we can only keep a firm grip on this bold confidence, we're the house! That's why the Holy Spirit says, today, please listen; don't turn a deaf ear as in "the bitter uprising," that time of wilderness testing! Even though they watched me at work for forty years, your ancestors refused to let me do it my way; over and over they tried my patience. And I was provoked, oh, so provoked! I said, "They'll never keep their minds on God; they refuse to walk down my road." Exasperated, I vowed, "They'll never get where they're going, never be able to sit down and rest."
>
> Hebrews 3:6-11 (MSG)

What did it feel like in those times of your life where you walked in circles?

_____

_____

List the steps you need to implement in your life to find your bearings and fulfill the purpose and destiny you were created for.

What things God had in store for you do you think were delayed as you tried to find your way?

# UNDESERVING

Your love is as real as the
   warmth from the sun
Your mercy as endless as
   this race that I run
Your unceasing grace I
   cannot fathom
Your whispers echo deeper
   than the darkest of chasms
Your mighty arm is stretched to
   this earth from your throne
Constantly guiding me
I'm never left alone
Your ways are inscribed in
   the heart of this man
My soul you've claimed by
   the palm of your hands
You call me your treasure
Yet I'm rich because of you
I'm your beloved
Yet you're the one who
   remains faithful and true
In my eyes I'm a failure
Success lies unseen

**DAY 22**

> Yet you see only my accomplishments
> And every one of my dreams
> It breaks my heart to know
> > you died for all
> Yet so many trash their life
> Help me to not be one
> That wastes your perfect sacrifice

God is so amazing; he is so good to us. He is everything to me, even when I do absolutely nothing for him. It is impossible for me to know all that he has done for me and even more impossible for me to understand why. Who else do you know that would love you so much though you have done nothing at all to deserve that love? He died on the cross for you and me, which is amazing all by itself. He tells us how good we are, how much he loves us, and all that we are to him, yet I can't remember being that good, loving him that much, or attempting to be anything at all to him. I am now trying to be those things, but he told me, long before it was even a thought in my mind. My, how good he is to an undeserving world. I can't help but feel like what he did for us was a waste when we don't even acknowledge who he is. I wonder if he ever feels like he should have just gotten rid of us all and started over, like he did in Noah's day and age. Yet I know it's never crossed his mind. Why? Well, because he loves us so much. Thank you, Lord, that you treat an undeserving people as if they deserve it all.

> We believe that we are all saved the same way, by the undeserved grace of the Lord Jesus.
>
> Acts 15:11 (NLT)

What does it mean to you for God to love you even though you don't deserve it?

_____

_____

_____

_____

How can you extend his love for you to others? How can you show people the love of Christ?

_____

_____

_____

_____

God loves you the way you are. What kind of person were you when you accepted his love?

_____

_____

_____

_____

# INSEPARABLE

Though I ran from you
You never left my side
Though I hurt you so
 many times
You never let me cry
Though I've sacrificed you
 over and over again
You still won't allow me to die
You're a merciful loving God
Who will never forsake me
I don't deserve you
Yet you freely give
 yourself to me
When I should have been
 long forgotten
And left alone
You still called my heart
 your home
My life you continue to hold
No matter the circumstance
When I fall flat on my face
I still receive from you
 another chance
There's no one like you

**DAY 23**

> And there will never be
> For as much love as you have given
> I desire to return to thee

I love to read these words that are written here on this paper. They are so powerful to my own life, and they portray the goodness and faithfulness of God to his children. Do you understand that we don't deserve who he has been and is to us? But does it matter to him? Not at all. He loves us no less today than he did the day before. God should have left me by the wayside, though I'm so grateful that he didn't. He has been the complete opposite to me of what I have been and done to him in this life. I ran from him in certain things in my life, but when I looked around, he was still there. Though I hurt him over and over again, I know that he hates it when I'm hurt and sad.

He is a merciful, loving God, and he will never forsake you. No matter what you do, he will always accept you. God has shown me more love than I have ever deserved and certainly more than I have ever imagined someone could show me. Because of what he has done and given me, I will do my best to do what he asks me to and serve him with my whole life. I know I can't give him what he's given me, but he doesn't expect me to. He just wants our best, and even if he doesn't get that, it won't change anything. He will always be proud of us and will always love us.

> And having chosen them, he called them to come to him. And having called them, he gave them right standing with himself. And having given them right standing, he gave them his glory. What shall we say about such wonderful things as these? If God is for us, who can ever be against us? Since he did not spare even his own Son but gave him up for us all, won't he also give us everything else?
>
> Romans 8:30-32 (NLT)

How do you feel knowing that nothing can separate you from the love of God?

_____

_____

_____

_____

How can this fact make you fall in love with him even more and push you to please him in all that you do?

_____

_____

_____

_____

Referring to the Bible verse above, other than his own son, what are some other things God has given us?

_____

_____

_____

_____

# DON'T LET GO

> Yea though I walk
>    through the valley
> Of the shadow of hurt
> I will not turn away
> I will stand firm, lift up my eyes,
> And this I'll pray
> That you would protect
>    and restore
> Keep my feet on solid rock
> And far from life's shore
> Remind me of your faithfulness,
>    mercy, and grace
> And renew my strength
> To run this race
> Mend me of this brokenness
> And shelter me from the rain
> As I grip your promise
> That exceeds all my pain

**DAY 24**

Life can be a cruel thing; life can be unfair. If we lived life just accepting what came our way, we would be so beat down and ragged that we'd just give up. If we all lived with that whatever-will-be-will-be mentality, there would be no hope in this world. I'm thankful that I have something bigger than this life that leads and guides me. In today's society where everything is so negative, with job unemployment skyrocketing, crime increasing, sickness and diseases on the rise, so many live in fear about what is going to happen tomorrow. When tomorrow arrives and is cruel and unfair, so many just say, "Oh well, what can I do?" I refuse to be one of those people! I refuse to let life choose my destiny when my destiny was chosen before my life even began. Your destiny includes the promises of God. He has promised things to you through his unfailing Word that overcomes all things. Grip those promises in your hand and don't let them go. Look life in the face and tell it you refuse to accept what contradicts your promise. You will see that, through his Word and by your faith in those promises, he will take care of you.

> Therefore I tell you, do not worry about your life, what you will eat or drink; or about your body, what you will wear. Is not life more important than food, and the body more important than clothes? Look at the birds of the air; they do not sow or reap or store away in barns, and yet your heavenly Father feeds them. Are you not much more valuable than they? Who of you by worrying can add a single

hour to his life? And why do you worry about clothes? See how the lilies of the field grow. They do not labor or spin. Yet I tell you that not even Solomon in all his splendor was dressed like one of these. If that is how God clothes the grass of the field, which is here today and tomorrow is thrown into the fire, will he not much more clothe you, O you of little faith? So do not worry, saying, "What shall we eat?" or "What shall we drink?" or "What shall we wear?" For the pagans run after all these things, and your heavenly Father knows that you need them. But seek first his kingdom and his righteousness, and all these things will be given to you as well. Therefore do not worry about tomorrow, for tomorrow will worry about itself. Each day has enough trouble of its own.

Matthew 6:25-34 (NIV)

What promises has God made to you that you are holding tightly to?

_____

_____

Describe a way his promises brought you victory when you didn't let go of what he said.

How can you remind yourself every day that you don't have to accept what life gives you but you can believe what God has promised?

# NONE LIKE HIM

Who is like you, Lord?
I could search for eternity
And find no one
Who compares to your beauty
I could search through all the ages
And find no one
Who is as perfect and
 flawless as my Lord
I could search to the
 ends of the earth
And not find one thing
 to compare to him
What words could I use
 to describe him?
I could learn every language
 ancient and new
Yet never find the right
 word to describe him
He surpasses all human intellect
He is a treasure that some
 will never know
He is perfect, peaceful, flawless,
 righteous, magnificent,

**DAY 25**

Mighty, gentle, loving, kind, caring,
Jealous, compassionate, and more
He is the King of Kings
And Lord of Lords
There is no one like him
And there will never be
Lord, I thank you so much
For who you are to me
How wonderful your holy presence
Such peace and rest do I find there
How awesome the touch of your hand
You restore my ruins taking
    every worry and care
Better is one day in your courts
Than a thousand elsewhere
Better is one second with my Jesus
Than for me to be anywhere else on earth
I declare all your works
I brag about your matchless worth
For who is like you?
Whose breath alone creates life?
Whose very voice thunders the heavens?
Who took the darkness
    and formed light?
Who holds our hopes, dreams,
    plans, and souls in his hand?

> Who dug the oceans, carved
>     the mountains,
> And placed every star
>     throughout the land?
> Only the King of Glory, the
>     Lord of creation
> Only my hope, my strength,
>     my savior, my friend
> The only one whose love,
>     grace, and mercy
> Endures to the end

It never ceases to amaze me that the awesome, all-knowing, all-powerful creator of heaven and earth is my friend! There is no one like him; no one can love like he does. No one can forgive like he does. No one can encourage, heal, restore, teach, and care like he does. He is matchless in his ways and can do whatever he wants to, yet he chose to have a relationship with me! The God that can do anything longs to just be with me and with you! Not because we are so great, but because he is so great, because his love is so great. We are the apples of his eye, the joys of his heart, and I know there's nothing he would rather do than be with us, to walk with us and talk with us, pick us up when we fall, cheer for us, encourage us, laugh with us, cry with us, and just be near us. He loves us so much and not because of what we do but because he is love. With him in my corner, how can I fail? How can you fail? Allow the God above every god to do what he does best; allow him to love you. Let him take your life and make something worth living out of it. Let the incomparable God give you an incomparable life.

> There's no one quite like you among the gods, O Lord, and nothing to compare with your works. All the nations you made are on their way, ready to give honor to you, O Lord, ready to put your beauty on display, parading your greatness, and the great things you do—God, you're the one, there's no one but you!
>
> Psalm 86:8 (MSG)

List some qualities that God holds that no one in your life can match.

_____

_____

_____

_____

Letting an incomparable God have control in your life has changed your life in what ways?

_____

_____

_____

_____

What can you do differently to help open people's eyes to the amazing God you serve?

_____

_____

_____

_____

# MY ENEMY

For every deed and every fault
Every single sin I've ever thought
For every mistake and
    failure I've realized
There's no one to blame
For these doings were all mine
I'm the one who makes me fall
Though I should be running
I'm the one who makes me crawl
I'm the reason I can't stand tall
I'm the one to blame
To blame for it all
Because I know
If I truly wanted to I
    could be free
So God
Keep me from myself
For I know my worst enemy
Is me

We've all heard it, and at one time we have all probably said it: "The devil made me do it." As easy as it is to blame our mistakes on others, especially the devil, it's just simply not true.

**DAY 26**

God gave all of us the same thing: free will. The devil can tempt me all he wants to, but the bottom line is that I still have to decide if I want to give in to temptation or not. Every day when we get up, we are faced with two choices: Am I going to be the lord of my life today, or am I going to let Jesus be the lord of my life today? I've discovered that when I choose to be lord, everything gets screwed up, yet I choose to be lord more often than I'd like to admit! Why is this? It's like telling the pilot of a plane that he needs to move because you want to fly, yet you've never flown a plane in your life. You know what that means, don't you? You're going to crash! The failures and mistakes, the wrong turns and dead-end streets I've ended up on in this life, are no one's fault but mine. My worst enemy in this life is none other than me.

> [I assure you] by the pride which I have in you in [your fellowship and union with] Christ Jesus our Lord, that I die daily [I face death every day and die to self].
>
> 1 Corinthians 15:31 (AMP)

In what ways do you need to guard yourself against yourself?

_____

_____

What are you doing to make sure you die daily, especially to the weaknesses in your life?

Dying to yourself means living in Christ wholly. What kind of impact do you think you can make when you allow Jesus to be lord of your life all the time?

# THE CHOICE IS YOURS

> There is a life I choose to live
> And walk in everyday
> A life that bears the fruit of love
> And stirs the hearts of all
> Who pass my way
> Kingdom minded in all I do
> Living for your name
> Standing out amongst the crowd
> I'm different from this world
> My life is not the same
> To live how you've called me to
> Is not an impossible thing
> It's just deciding to
> > make the choice
> It's a simple matter of discipline

One of the things that I struggle with most in my life is discipline. I struggle with it in all kinds of different areas. Reading the Bible and praying every day is a hard thing to do for me. I have to force myself at times to do them. If for some reason I miss a day, I'll end up missing three or four days at a time. I don't know why it's such a hardship for me to simply do these two things every day; perhaps we are all this way. I have to be careful, though, or I simply won't do it. Another area of my life that lacks discipline is eating healthy, which I know is something we all struggle with. I eat healthy and exercise for a little while and see great results. One day I let myself go and it's all over. I gain the weight back and lose the muscle mass I accrued—months of being on the right track to looking and feeling great gone from a simple lack of discipline. If you ask my wife, she will tell you I lack discipline in putting my dirty clothes in the hamper, and if you ask those who are around me regularly, they could probably think of something that I could improve on through discipline.

Discipline is the key to a successful life. Discipline can keep you on the right track and off the wrong ones. A simple means of discipline in your life can keep you far from sin. Discipline can keep you out of financial trouble, help promote a healthy life, and be the tool that promotes you in your job and in God's kingdom. I think discipline is too important to be overlooked in our lives and needs to be something we use with pride. If we can't be disciplined in our own lives, how can we disciple others?

> No discipline seems pleasant at the time, but painful. Later on, however, it produces a harvest of righteousness and peace for those who have been trained by it.
>
> Hebrews 12:11 (NIV)

What areas of your life lack discipline?

_____

_____

_____

_____

What are some ways you reinforce the necessity for discipline in your daily life?

_____

_____

_____

_____

How can you keep yourself focused on those areas you need work in to not let discipline fall short?

_____

_____

_____

_____

# CONFESSIONS

I am blessed coming in
    and going out
I'm the head and not the tail
I'm above and not beneath
I'm more than a conqueror
I cannot fail
You've ordered my steps
You guide me today
Your word is a lamp
    lighting the way
Wisdom's my sister
Understanding's my friend
I'm free from all harm
By the angels you send
By your stripes I am healed
By your grace I am free
Over this world through
    my faith
I walk in victory
I find favor with you
And even with man
Since you are for me
Who against me can stand

**DAY 28**

> All that you are I personify today
> I'm a shining light to every dark place
> Strengthening my life
> And this faith I possess
> Every day over myself
> Your Word I confess

Several years ago I was taught to do something that has changed my spiritual living. I was taught to put into practice a daily confession of God's Word over my life. The poem you have just read is a clip of what I pray over myself and my family every day. It's really nothing out of the ordinary; everything in that poem is a verse from the Bible. So what is a confession? Simply saying about yourself what God says about you! I take the truths of God's Word and the promises he has given to me and I speak them over my life. This practice has two benefits: I say God's Word, therefore, hearing God's Word and building faith in my life (Romans 10:17). Also, by building faith in my life, I'm securing victory over what this world is dishing out (1 John 5:4). This isn't some miracle chant to make all things go away. You will still face problems as normal, but you will already have the faith you need working through you to overcome those obstacles in your life.

Let me give you an example. I have two wonderful boys who are now six and two years old. Both are as healthy as they can be, and I thank God every day for their healthy bodies, but when each of them was born, they had some complications. Both spent a week in the NICU upon arrival. Noah, my oldest, had breathing complications. The doctors and nurses said that he had fluid in his lungs. Judah, my youngest son, was having what the doctors called "seizures." He even had to see a neurologist, who ran tests on his brain. With both of our children, my wife and I didn't panic; we knew that everything was going to be just fine. From the moment we discovered that we were going to have a child, we began to thank God for a wonderful healthy baby. We would say every day, "God, we thank you for a beautiful healthy baby, free from all sickness and disease, because by your son Jesus's stripes, he is healed" (Isaiah 53:5). We built up our faith for the believing of healthy children, so when the enemy tried to attack us with negative news, the faith we needed was already at work in our lives and brought us the victory. Now I'm not saying that they were healed of major issues or that had we not done that, things would have turned out differently. To be honest, I don't know what the outcome would have been. I simply chose to take control of their lives through faith before any situations presented themselves. This is how I choose to begin each day. I have, through personal experiences, found it to make my life and my journey with God better.

> It is written: "I believed; therefore I have spoken." With that same spirit of faith we also believe and therefore speak.
>
> 2 Corinthians 4:13 (NIV)

Name some scriptures that are important to you regarding God's promises for your life.

_____

_____

_____

_____

What events in your life do you think would have turned out differently had you been building up your faith through confessing God's Word?

_____

_____

_____

_____

What steps can you take to ensure you pray those scriptures listed above over you and your family every day?

_____

_____

_____

_____

# HEAVEN'S SAKE

How will I live life today
What will I do
Do I live this life for me today
Or do I live this life for you
There's a purpose for me today
And it goes beyond any career
There's a destiny for me today
But will I realize
That the day of destiny is here
So many will live their life today
For no one but themselves
I choose to live this life today
Giving of myself
To those that are hurt
    and those in need
That we come across everyday
Let me give what's inside of me
Let me give Jesus away
We have become a selfish people
All we do is take
But I choose to not
    live for myself
I choose to live for heaven's sake

**DAY 29**

I like stuff—cars, clothes, boats, houses, golf clubs, and especially money! I don't want these things to drive my life, though. All of them are good, but they should be at the bottom of the list. Retirement, college funds, investment opportunities—they are great ideas that I plan to have, but I'm not living my life for a comfortable final few years on earth; I'm living for the endless years that follow. I want my kids to get a good education, and I want them to have a good career, but I'd rather teach them how to expand the kingdom of heaven. If I had to choose between them learning how to give generously and be a blessing or how to invest in stock options for a comfortable future, I'd choose being a blessing every time. I hope they learn both, but only one will matter in the end. I want to teach my boys to throw a football so one day they can be the quarterbacks of their high school teams. But more than that, I want to teach them how to make a difference so they can show the hurting world around them that God loves them and that his son, Jesus, died for them. I want to give my life away to missions, my church, my family, and my community. I want to be an example of who Christ was and is to my wife, my children, my friends, my coworkers, and anybody else I come across in my daily life. I don't want to live for the selfishness that has fueled this world's passion for life. I want to live below my means financially and with the time I'm given every day so I can bless those who need blessed and give of myself to those who need help. We try to spend a million dollars on a thousand-dollar budget and live thirty hours in a twenty-four-hour day. We are left with no resources for kingdom issues. One day the house will fall apart, the car will break down, and the clothes will be tattered, and people will still be hurting. We all have lived, and the majority still does, for our own sakes, but I wonder what would happen if we all decided to live for the sake of heaven. I plan to; what about you?

> Even though I am free of the demands and expectations of everyone, I have voluntarily become a servant to any and all in order to reach a wide range of people: religious, nonreligious, meticulous moralists, loose-living immoralists, the defeated, the demoralized-whoever. I didn't take on their way of life. I kept my bearings in Christ-but I entered their world and tried to experience things from their point of view. I've become just about every sort of servant there is in my attempts to lead those I meet into a God-saved life. I did all this because of the

Message. I didn't just want to talk about it; I wanted to be in on it!

1 Corinthians 9:19-23 (MSG)

Evaluate the important things in your life. How many of those things are for your own cause?

_____

_____

_____

_____

What needs to change so that you live for the sake of heaven and not for your own?

_____

_____

_____

_____

Your few short years on earth determine how you will live the eternal years afterward. Understanding this, what priorities need to shift in your life?

_____

_____

_____

_____

# THE JOURNEY OF LIFE

As I stand on this mountain
    I peer over the edge
Down below I see a
    beautiful valley
Yet it's the valley of death
I see below me the familiar
    places where I stopped to rest
I see the traces of rockslides
And the memories of when I fell
    back to the places I once left
I see how far I've come
How far you've brought
    me from the start
I see the days I pleased you
But I also see the days I
    broke your heart
I see the days I camped out
Because I didn't think I
    could go on anymore
And I see the days I went
    leaps and bounds

> Over boulders and rocks for
>     your cause, oh Lord
> I see the hurt, pain, and all the storms
> Still I see the joy that comes
>     with the sunshine
> Of every new morn
> I see those times I sat and
>     cried in all my failures
> And yet I see when your
>     hand came down
> And pulled me to shelter
> I see every past circumstance
>     in my life up to now
> Yet I look up and see the
>     rest of the climb
> And all I can think is how
> But you haven't left me yet
> Not even in the midst of my sorrow
> So keep me safe tonight and
>     renew my strength
> For my journey tomorrow

I think the journey of everyone's life can be summed up right here. If someone could paint a picture of your climb through life, this is probably what it would look like. I know mine would.

As I look down over the edge now in my life, I can see where I started. I lived in the valley where all the unbelievers lived. From here, it looks so beautiful, but I remember the hopelessness that I felt trying what the world had to offer and never being satisfied. I see where the rocks gave way as I slid back to the valley over and over again. What a long way down it is now. I see all the people God used me to minister to, the great things I've been a part of for his name. There mixed in I also see those times I did my own things, pleasing my own fleshly desires when I didn't put him first. There are so many of those places along the path. I see where I was satisfied with where I was and didn't feel like pushing on and the places where I was too scared to go on so I just stayed there. My, what time has been wasted there at those campsites. If I had just pushed on, then I'd be so much higher now. I see the struggles I've faced along this mountainside and where I stopped to feel sorry for myself. But I can still see where God didn't give up on me but encouraged and carried me through those problems. I can see and remember all the circumstances that life has brought my way, but what an amazing, good life God has given me through grace. I still have a long way to go, but as I think about it now, there's no way I can ask, "How?" I know how; the same way I have done it all these years—with his Word and his spirit that he has placed inside me.

I know a lot of you can look back over life and find similar circumstances that have occurred along the way. Try to imagine your journey. What does it look like? I know it's challenging and it's not that life should be difficult or hard because it shouldn't be, especially when you take God at his Word. But it is a climb. You have to go against the flow and rise above the rest when you begin this journey. At times it may appear difficult; it's not for the wimpy, that's for sure. It is for those who won't back down, who aren't afraid to stand when there's nothing to stand on but faith. Now that's a challenge. I've never regretted starting this journey in life, rising higher and higher as I grow in God's Word. No, I've never regretted it. I've loved it. I can't wait to go to sleep tonight so I can rise, with his help, a little higher tomorrow.

> Your life is a journey you must travel with a deep consciousness of God. It cost God plenty to get you out of that dead-end, empty-headed life you grew up in. He paid with Christ's sacred blood, you know. He died like an unblemished, sacrificial lamb. And this was no afterthought. Even though it has only lately—at the end of the ages—become public

knowledge, God always knew he was going to do this for you. It's because of this sacrificed Messiah, whom God then raised from the dead and glorified, that you trust God, that you know you have a future in God.

1 Peter 1:18-21 (MSG)

Looking back over your climb, what does it look like? What do you see?

_____

_____

_____

_____

Think of your future. It looks better than anything you have experienced yet. What are you going to do differently tomorrow to make sure that success is certain?

_____

_____

_____

_____

It cost God a lot to get you off the road you were on. How can you live the best life possible to honor his sacrifice?

_____

_____

_____

_____

# CONCLUSION

This book will have only been successful if it helps you on your journey. I can tell you God loves you even though you don't deserve it. I can remind you how important it is to read your Bible and do what it says. I can encourage you to pray and begin to build a relationship with God every day. I can warn you about trying to live life on your own without God in it. But if you don't apply these simple truths, the journey that you live and the roads you travel will never change. Stop being someone who just hears God's Word; start being someone who does what God's Word says. In order to get different results, you have to do something different.

I'm not perfect by any means. I simply want the best life I can have. I want to live the God life he intended me to live. I want to experience that abundant life Jesus said he came to give us. If you apply these life truths and begin to practice them daily, then we can journey together. Make a decision today to unsubscribe yourself to the dull, boring, lifeless road you are on. Take the next exit and get on God's highway. Life is so much better here! I believe God blesses us for one reason: so that we can bless others. I hope that through the blessings he has given me, I have blessed you and your life.

"Therefore everyone who hears these words of mine and puts them into practice is like a wise man who built his house on the rock."

Matthew 7:24 (NIV)

## UNSUBSCRIBE ME

### FROM A MUNDANE LIFE ON THIS WORLD'S DEAD-END ROAD

Beginning today, ___/___/___ (month, day, year)

I will not live life to simply exist. I am making a conscious and permanent decision to fulfill the God-given purpose and destiny that I was created for. I choose to subscribe myself to the abundant life that Jesus has to offer and allow God's spirit and his Word to lead me down the road of faith, hope, and love.

Signature _____

# Some Important Sayings

★. Never make an important decision in a hurry take your time till you have peace about it.

★. Never let anybody control you or your spirit.

★. Make new friends and keep the old (if you can) One is Silver & the other is Gold.

★. Never holler at anybody unless the house is on fire -

★.